Women' of Ministry

Images from Scripture

Pauline Warner

Methodist Minister, Coventry

GROVE BOOKS LIMITED
BRAMCOTE NOTTINGHAM NG9 3DS

Contents

The Cover Illustration is by Peter Ashton

First Impression December 1994
ISSN 0144-171X
ISBN 1 85174 282 4

1
Introduction

Icons are pictures which point beyond the images on the surface to eternal truths. I want to present several biblical characters as icons. Most of them are of women and I want to paint the icons of these women from a woman's point of view to exhibit a whole new perspective so that we see these people through new eyes. I believe that this will inspire and challenge at a particularly creative and difficult time in the history of the church.

An Icon of Change: Peter and Cornelius

Peter was staying at the house of Simon the tanner when he received a vision from God which changed his life and the direction of the early church (Acts 10.1-16). Through the vision he was commanded to eat those very animals which he, as a Jew, had always been forbidden to eat. Initially Peter was perturbed by the meaning of the vision. It was interpreted for him by the events which followed immediately afterwards. The servants of Cornelius, the God-fearing gentile who had also received a vision from God, arrived to take Peter to their master. This began the mission to, and by, the gentiles. The Christian movement broke out of (or at least was moved out of) its exclusively Jewish background and the gentiles were recognised as equal partners in the work of sharing the gospel of Jesus Christ.

That story at Joppa expresses something of the turmoil which all the first Christians, not just Peter, must have gone through as they were made to come to terms with God not only working through people who were not of the chosen people, the Jews, but also in ways which seemed contradictory to what they had always been taught to be the law of God.

Today the Church stands at a similar turning point. The story of the tension between Jew and Gentile rings many bells but now the issue is about men and women. The question faced by the first Christians was how much those Gentiles had to become Jews first and obedient to the traditions and customs of the Jewish religion. The issue many Christian women now feel is how much do we have to become masculine first and accept masculine perspectives and behaviour. Or are we allowed to be truly distinctive and offer gifts and attitudes which are different from the men's? If that is to happen, women must be able to feel that everything they say or do does not have to pass through the judgement of men—just as the gentiles in Galatia had to feel free not to have to pass through the rite of circumcision.

There is obviously not enough space to enter into a detailed discussion of these issues in this booklet. They have, in any case, been well rehearsed elsewhere. The point I am making is simply that the story of Joppa is a useful icon of change among Christians because it reminds us that there must always be a tension between tradition and innovation. Perhaps it would help if I sketched a picture of myself so that you can get some idea of the perspective from which I write.

I am an ordained Methodist minister who believes in the authority of Scripture and has a great deal of respect for the Catholic teaching both about priesthood and the traditional role of women because I perceive that it contains a spiritual depth which our generation is prone to miss. I also write as a woman who has been greatly helped in my own journey by the ideas of the feminist movement and, although I would not go along entirely with a secular feminist approach, I cannot but honour that particular sphere of influence.

I write as a minister who time and again has listened to women expressing variations on the same theme, which was most succinctly put by one woman: 'I am a committed Christian. I know that God is my Father and Jesus is my saviour and brother. I am not interested in feminist re-writings of the faith which want to call God 'Mother'. But the church won't listen to my womanhood.'

I write as a Christian increasingly caught up in a movement of the Spirit in which women are being empowered and liberated and which has led many people to be convinced that God is calling us to a new Joppa where traditional Christianity which has been sincerely and obediently interpreted mainly by men for two thousand years must allow itself to be changed by the new apostles who have a very different way of looking at the world. Yet these women, who are so obviously being filled with the Spirit, must also acknowledge with humility that the past traditions and teaching need to be respected as God's chosen way of grace. Otherwise we could deny God's revelation of himself in Jesus Christ. Mutual listening, submission and delight are required now as they were in Joppa and Jerusalem.

Lastly, I write as someone who is increasingly convinced that stereotypes of what is male and female are not very helpful. In my life, I have been grateful for male friends who have taught me to be gentle and imaginative. I am equally grateful to women who taught me how to be assertive and logical. It is perhaps inevitable that certain characteristics will continue to be referred to as 'feminine' and some as 'masculine'. However, I feel that it is increasingly recognised that all human beings have both parts to their personality. So, as I sketch these icons I do not intend to imply that the characteristics discerned in these biblical women apply only to women. They may well be feminine but can equally well be found in men. I hope that men who ponder these pictures will be able to reflect on the feminine side of their own personalities.

The questions have been included to encourage you to think and discuss.

Please treat this book rather like a photo album and flick through the set of pictures, stopping to ponder in more detail when one of the pictures catches your eye. You are entirely free to argue that you do not agree with the angle from which the picture was taken and that you don't think it does the person justice!

2

Mary and Elizabeth

I have learned one thing above all in my ministry to, and with, women. Our cardinal sin is not pride but self-deprecation. Nowhere is the difference between men's and women's perspectives more striking than in this. Every single woman I have counselled has needed to be built up in confidence and given a sense of self worth. When I lead a prayer of confession in church now, I never mention 'pride' without simultaneously mentioning 'lack of confidence' because I know that too many women are like frightened creatures who, just daring to wake up, are suddenly startled back through fear and guilt.

The story of the visitation, of Mary visiting Elizabeth's house, is a beautiful icon of women as sisters in God, giving that confidence and encouragement to one another. They delight in each other's worth and recognise the promises of God bestowed on one another. They also show a proper sense of self-worth. Mary is able to say: 'The Almighty has done great things for me.' Her identity is grounded in God's love and action. This is not a self-esteem deriving from her own greatness but an acknowledgement of God's love. It is thus truly humble. This is not the same as 'humiliation'. Women often confuse the two words because they have been made to feel arrogant if they are assertive or confident. Mary shows strength in many ways, not least in her capacity to receive affirmation.

We sometimes forget that it was only within the union of this fellowship that Mary was able to give full vent to praise in the Magnificat. Her first action after the visit of the angel was to reach out to another person. Women need mutual support and encouragement and are as likely to find it in the mutual exchange of human relationship as in the church building or organisation. Mary did not hasten to the synagogue to give praise. She turned to another human being in her home who responded to her at a level deeper than words.

As soon as Mary enters Elizabeth's house, her cousin instinctively recognises why she has come and does not need to be told. Elizabeth is the first human being to recognise the reality of the angel's words and call Mary 'The mother of the Lord'. She recognised the Christ in her and affirmed Mary's calling.

No-one but Mary will ever again carry God incarnate within her but in our own way we do all bear Christ and bring him forth for the world. We need companions and friends to share with for they will discern and encourage those first signs of growth in us (and we in them). The true friend sees more in us than we see and delights in what she senses. Elizabeth did not have to be told why she had come. She knew instinctively. She knew because the baby leapt in her womb. 'Gut reaction' is women's mode of knowing. This gut reaction, like Mary's strength, does not come from herself alone but from her closeness to God. She seems to be one of those women who can so easily recognise God in others precisely because they are so full of his gracious nature themselves.

The original word 'gossip' did not mean malevolent talkers but 'God siblings'. In particular gossips were women who shared with a woman during her pregnancy, childbirth and the first weeks of the baby's life. Like many words to do with women it has become debased (you have only to reflect what the word 'master' conveys compared to the word 'mistress'). Gossip was originally, then, chatter about new life shared in very ordinary and busy situations. A brilliant example of the real meaning of gossip was given recently when Abbie Humphreys, the baby abducted from hospital straight after her birth, was found through the intuition of women who said that they were 'proud to be gossips'. Their instincts and experience of pregnancy and childbirth succeeded where the logical approach of the professionals had failed.

Similarly, many women believe that the best way of spreading the good news of God's bringing people to new life is in the ordinary exchanges of everyday life. Gossiping the gospel, like Mary and Elizabeth, they reach out to each other in need and joy and recognise in each other the amazing things which God is doing.

3
Mary at Pentecost

If this booklet is a snapshot album, then I have to be honest and say that the next picture is not one which I have taken. It is a very old picture and I include it for that very reason. It is the traditional icon, used by the Roman Catholic and Eastern Orthodox churches, of Pentecost. As the apostles receive the Holy Spirit, Mary is there in the centre of them.

As I explained in the introduction, this booklet aims to encourage a mutual submission between tradition and innovation. So I include this particular icon as a way of honouring the tradition of the Roman Catholic church. The explanation of it was given to me by a Roman Catholic priest and may seem strange to Protestants who may well want to say 'Where does it say this in the Bible?' The truth is that the Catholic tradition is rather like Mary, who took the words which were spoken about Jesus and 'pondered them in her heart' (Luke 2.19). Much of their tradition comes from that deep reflection over many years. I believe that such slow pondering is the way that many women know and experience their life and faith. Of course there are limitations to this way of knowing as there are dangers in adding too much tradition to the scriptural foundation. Nevertheless there is a validity to this pondering approach and I ask you to use it as you browse over this particular icon.

In any case the idea that Mary was there on the day of Pentecost is not entirely unreasonable. It is inferred from the Acts of the Apostles chapter 1 verse 14 which describes the apostles at prayer 'together with the women and Mary, the mother of Jesus, and with his brothers'. Chapter 2 verse 1, in describing the day of Pentecost, says that 'they were all together in one place'. If the words 'all together' is taken to refer to that previous description of the expectant apostles, it is not unreasonable to assume that Mary and the other women were there on that day.

This icon, then, pictures Mary at the centre with the apostles looking towards her as the Holy Spirit descends. This is the beginning of the church and there, in the middle of the male apostles, is this elderly woman. They look to her as one who can teach them because she knows what it is like to receive the Spirit and live a Spirit-filled life. She has been doing so for the past thirty four or so years since the Spirit overshadowed her (Luke 1.26-38). She really is the mother of the church, the one who can educate and nurture them through her love and her experience.

Glancing back to the annunciation story and what followed, we can see that Mary's example teaches that the nature of a Spirit-filled life is a complete surrender to God without asking to know the details. She was prepared to leave the future open and wait on God's timing and will. At times she frankly did not know what was going on but still she was obedient. At times the family life was fractured and human relationships put at risk but still she stayed obedient.

Previous generations to our own, recognising her openness to God, described her as 'the empty vessel of grace'. She was empty of anything which would block the Holy Spirit from entering her; her fears about the future, her concern at what other people would say, her doubts and disbelief, her self-sufficiency, her lack of confidence. Whatever it was that could block the Spirit, Mary was free from these. So the Spirit could enter into her and inwardly conceive the Christ child. As in any pregnancy, the initial changes were not noticeable, perhaps not even to the mother herself. But then the inward changes became stronger and more evident to those outside until she reached a point where she could not hold herself back but would have to share Christ with the world.

Her example is an example to us all, male or female. We all need to be empty before the Lord, empty that the Spirit might enter into our hearts and conceive the Christ within us. Changes may be slow and imperceptible but, if we allow the Spirit to continue to nurture, there will come a time when 'necessity will be laid upon us' and we will have to bring forth Christ to share him with the world. If we allow that to happen we truly become Christ-bearers for one another. As the apostles receive the Spirit they begin a new phase of their lives in which they will be called to give up safe surroundings, in which relationships will be strained through loyalty to Christ, where they will be derided and rejected and they will know times when they simply do not understand what God is doing. They will thus benefit by Mary's example of complete self-giving to God.

Mary's example teaches the disciples (as presumably she taught her growing son) that to live life in the Spirit means a willingness to be used by God as he wills. She showed this attitude consistently. We see it again at the foot of the cross when once again she allows her future life to be decided by God through his son.(John 19.26-27). It is this willingness-to-be-disposed of by God which characterises all Christian discipleship. It is what Mary teaches so clearly by her example. At every stage of our lives we must say 'Lord let it be unto me according to your will'. And we do not need to ask for the details!

This icon is particularly important because it transcends the stereotypes of womanhood. Traditionally the church has tended to portray women as in the background. Now we rightly emphasise the strength of women and their right to be actively involved in the church. Yet gospel values must make us wary of emphasising an assertiveness which is self-centred and self-seeking. After all, Christ, who is the person in the universe with the most power and right to be at the centre of attention, freely chose to become a servant. There is nothing wrong or second-best about being in the background. It is to be truly Christ-like.

Mary must have been a very strong woman to have been able to handle so much in her life. Yet she was prepared to stay in the background. The vast majority of her vocation was lived in the anonymity of an ordinary village, away from the public view. It was there that she fulfilled the most important task that was ever laid on a woman—to nurture and bring up the son of God. I believe that the whole church needs to ponder her story more deeply (including those thirty or so years in Nazareth) because it is so challenging to our idea of what it is to be a woman. In the one hand, she challenges the idea (so often presented by the church in the past) that women are weak and helpless. On the other hand, she challenges the modern idea that the only way to be of value is to be 'up-front'.

In recent years there has been a great deal written about the women of the Bible and the church. We have been made to recognise how much they have been neglected in the preaching and teaching of the church. I am in total agreement with such a movement but want to register a concern that if we take it too far we can focus on the women for women's sake and not for Christ's sake. This is why Mary is such an important icon for the whole church. Everything she did was to point away from herself to her son. This traditional icon of Mary at Pentecost places a woman in the centre not for her own sake but because she has lived a life which has been God-centred. This is what she had to teach the newly inspired apostles and what she can teach the church today.

4
The Women at the Foot of the Cross

According to John, Mary was standing by the foot of the cross (John 19.25) along with her sister and Mary Magdalene. The other evangelists also speak of the women disciples being there (Matthew 28.55-56; Mark 15.40-41; Luke 23.49). The names of the women vary but one detail does not. They are described as 'standing at a distance'.

Our next icon is nothing but a quick snapshot of that scene at the cross. I want to suggest that as Mary at Pentecost can serve as an icon for the whole church's openness to receive the Spirit, so the women at the cross can serve as an icon for the priesthood of all believers.

This booklet has been timed to coincide with the expansion of women's ministry to the ordained priesthood. I do not intend to discuss the various theologies of ordination and ministry to be found in the church but surely all denominations and traditions would agree that the primary calling of ordained ministers is not to 'have authority' nor 'hold responsibility' but humbly point to the saving grace of the Saviour's death.

The women who stood at a distance express the rightful distance between ourselves and 'the one true, perfect, immortal sacrifice'. Once again, the picture of Mary is particularly powerful for as the mother of Jesus she would have felt his every agony as those nails were driven into his hands. She would have shared deeply in his sufferings but the fact is that she did not actually feel the torture nor was it her hands that were pierced. She did not actually die the death that would redeem humanity. She and the other women were there not as the saviour of the world but as ones who stood and watched.

So are we. When the community of believers gathers to celebrate that death, we do not do so to save ourselves. Priest and people can get no nearer than 'standing at a distance' and watch the only redeemer.

5
The Hebrew Midwives

Another word which has been debased in our language because of its close associations with womanly things is 'cunning'. It now carries connotations of deceit, but they were not there originally. It is derived from the Latin cunnus meaning 'vagina', and is associated with Cunina (the Roman goddess who protects children in their cradle) whose name gave the word *cunabula* (which means 'cradle' or 'earliest abode'). It was also linked to the word *cunne* meaning 'to know' (as in 'Do you ken John Peel?'). Put all these together and the word 'cunning' originally meant something like 'knowing about, and being skilful in, womanly things'.

The Hebrew midwives of Exodus chapter 1 were definitely cunning women who used all their instinctive knowledge to outwit the oppressive Pharaoh. They did practice deceit, but it was done in order to protect life, and not through any cruel motive. They are our next icons.

In the first place, they highlight something about the need to confront injustice and cruelty wherever it is found. Women's work cannot be assigned to the home, nor Christian ministry to the sanctuary. Both must be exercised in the political sphere as well, and Christian women must not be made to feel unfeminine or unchristian exercising such a role. Wether it is lobbying an MP, active participation in local politics, or leading a Peace and Justice meeting at church, all these are appropriate, and indeed necessary, spheres of involvement for Christian women.

Secondly, the experience one woman shared with me recently has made me realise just how important an icon for ministry is provided by the work of midwives. She went away on a Christian weekend where pressure was put on her by one of the leaders who felt that she needed a deeper awareness of the Spirit. Several people prayed for her for quite a time but nothing happened. Eventually she used some of her cunning and pretended that it had, just to get some peace!

She told me that she had grown a lot more through reflecting on the experience than through the experience itself. The phrase that had been used was that she needed to be 'born again', a phase she had heard often but which struck her with a new force after that experience. In her own words, she said, 'Only men could talk about birth as if it were a quick thing, with an immediate change of 'before' and 'after'. Any woman knows that birth is long and slow, very painful and very messy. You expose the most embarrassing parts of yourself and are so vulnerable that you are past caring. If that is what real birth is like, then why should spiritual birth be any different?'

She then went on to reflect about her own process of giving birth where there had been two doctors who had given her instructions 'because they had read about birth in a book.' There had also been two midwives who had held her hands, mopped her brow, and occasionally given her advice. 'They were more help to me because they trusted me to know my own body and know what I could cope with at any one time.'

Her conclusion was that she had learned something of the nature of women's ministry. Women, knowing from their own experience that bodies work slowly and that emotions cannot be dealt with from a textbook, are less likely to give instructions and make decisions about how to be born again. Trust is the key word. The minister trusts the other person to know, under God, what she or he is able to cope with at that time. For, like midwives, they know that they are not responsible for creating the new life but only assisting in an important phase of its growing.

It is perhaps better to say that midwives are icons of a feminine approach to ministry which can equally well be exercised by men or women. There is a place for simply being with a person and letting them take their own time. Yet, on its own, that could easily become unhealthily passive and so there is also a place for a decisive ministry which challenges and confronts. That, as the Hebrew midwives show us, can equally well be exercised by women as well as men.

6
Ruth and Naomi

The relationship between Ruth and Naomi, her mother-in-law, is one of the loveliest in the Bible. Ruth's words of faithfulness and devotion speak of the relationship of intimacy and loyalty between women of different generations. However, it is not that relationship on which I want to focus. Rather, I want to consider Ruth and the man she eventually marries, Boaz. The fact that this part of the story is rarely emphasised speaks volumes for the attitude of the church towards the question of sex. Once when I was preaching on the story of Ruth, I looked for an abbreviated version so that the whole story could been read as the lesson. Not one of the simplified versions mentioned that Ruth had taken the initiative towards Boaz. Admittedly, most were written for children and they avoided the question altogether but even those which mentioned it phrased it in such a way as to suggest that Boaz had asked Ruth to marry him.

Ruth arrives in Bethlehem disinherited of any cultural identity. She has left her own country and people and yet she does not really belong to the people of her dead husband. She has no home and no status. Many women similarly feel that they are disinherited by the church because their womanhood has never been properly heeded and celebrated. The language and expressions of worship and the structures of the church feel so wrong. Nowhere is this more clearly seen than in the attitude towards female sexuality. Ever since Eve we seem to have been made to bear the shame of being sexual and especially for being the temptress that leads to man's downfall. This, in spite of the fact that there is absolutely no mention of sex anywhere in the Genesis story of the fall!

The issue of Christianity's attitude towards sexuality is not just a moral question about what is appropriate in physical relationships. The question of women's ordination has made this clear. 'I'm in favour of it and I shall not mind until we get a pretty priest. Then I will have difficulties,' said one man at a PCC meeting, as if this was an entirely rational argument! It seems that women are allowed to be mother figures, nurturing and caring and comforting. But a woman who is confident in being sensual causes problems. Moreover, she is the one who is made to feel guilty for being attractive and stirring the hang-ups of others!

This sense of being disinherited from their female identity has caused many women to turn away from the church. They do not need to look far to claim their female heritage because there is at the moment a whole explosion of interest in 'feminine consciousness' which is 'marketed' through the New Age and so-called 'alternative' groups. Such philosophies are usually based on the ideas of a matriarchal culture 'when God was a woman.' I believe that this whole area needs to be handled with sensitive pastoral and theological wisdom.

Many a woman has indeed been helped to discover her own femininity through the influence of these groups or the writing which comes out of them. It is not helpful to shout 'idolatry', 'heresy' or 'occult' at her. Indeed it is not helpful to shout at all; the aggressiveness of much evangelical Christianity is the very thing that has offended many and made the gentleness of New Age so attractive.

For example there are groups, called 'Maiden, Mother and Crone' workshops in which women are encouraged to explore their emotions at the various stages of their lives. Similar workshops called 'The Goddess Within' make the connection between parts of a woman's personality and stories of various goddesses. The 'Demeter side' is the mothering capacity of a woman, the 'Aphrodite side' her sexuality, the 'Athena side' her wisdom, and so on.

When a woman is helped to identify with these goddesses she is helped to come to terms with herself and become confident in her womanhood. She is not necessarily worshipping them. A lot of confusion and hurt would be overcome if we make it very clear that there is a difference between theology and psychology. The Great Goddess may not exist as the eternal deity but women feel these goddesses as archetypal figures within themselves. The wholesale denunciation of them has alienated many from Christianity because it has actually been an attack on their sense of womanhood.

Yet it is true that New Age and other related philosophies do indeed worship that which is less than God. The church must speak out against such blasphemy and offer appropriate spiritual guidance for individuals, particularly because there is a very fine line between such practices and the occult. Nevertheless, that is all the more reason to handle the question carefully. Insensitive dogmatism can actually turn a woman away from Christianity and catapult her into the very practices which the Church counsels against.

As women come to take a fuller part in the life of the church they can only do so if they are allowed to express their sexuality without shame or guilt. At worst, female sexuality has been dismissed as evil or at best kept under polite wraps. Until recently the chief end of marriage according to the Christian ceremony was procreation. Again, it seems that women are acceptable so long as they are useful in producing children. The sheer delight of surrendering to another in intimate union is not reason enough to marry or enjoy sex.

Yet marriage is one of the best icons of our union with God, as the Bible witnesses. 'As a bridegroom rejoices over the bride, so shall your God rejoice over you' (Isaiah 62.5). At least modern hymn writers enable us to respond with similar delight towards God: 'You alone are my heart's desire and I long to worship you'.

I think that we are only just beginning to come to terms what it means to call God 'husband'. It has hardly been used in mainstream Christianity. The mystical tradition has described 'the spiritual marriage' but since most mystics have also been celibate, the suspicion has been that such language comes out of sexual repression. I sense that such a suspicion is not entirely without justification and yet also not entirely fair! The phrase 'bride of Christ' has been used more widely but usually referring to the church as a whole and not individuals. The sexual implications are thereby avoided.

There is no space to explore all the implications of this biblical term. Some women will experience the love of God through the enfleshed reality of their earthly husband. Their husbands then become icons of God, of the God who liberates as well as the one who is authoritative. All people, women or men, married or single, know that the one to whom they are united first and foremost and in the deepest intimacy is God. The greatest commandment of all is 'You shall love the Lord your God with all your heart.'

When Ruth marries Boaz she does not only come into the heritage of the people of God. She herself becomes the agent of God's restoring love to that people and begins the messianic line which will descend through King David (Ruth 4.15-22). The previously disinherited Ruth became the agent of restoration. It may well be that Christian women who have felt for so long that they have had to deny such a fundamental aspect of their womanhood as their sexuality are now coming into their true feminine inheritance. If that is so, it will not only be themselves but the whole people of God who benefit, as the Lord restores all his people into a fulness of humanity.

7
Joseph

The mention of the husbandhood of God leads us to this next section in which in which we will consider the significance of Mary's earthly husband, Joseph, and his part within the relationship of the family at Nazareth.

Who held authority in that family? In a patriarchal society the wife and children would submit to the father and there is no reason to suppose that this did not happen in that family. Yet it is also clear that Joseph was prepared to take second place to his wife, recognising that her's was the superior vocation. He is prepared to let his life be disposed of by God in relation to Mary's calling and we hear hardly anything of him as he is prepared to take the subordinate role. Of course, it could be argued that both Joseph and Mary would submit to Jesus for they knew him to be the Messiah. Yet Luke tells us that 'he was obedient to them' (Luke 2.51).

The simplest answer is that no one person held authority for they all held it in a dynamic of mutual submission, each one recognising the other's distinct personality and vocation under God. I prefer not to say that no one person was the most important for that could make it sound as if everyone was levelled out in equal worthlessness. It is far more true to say that every single person was the most important because everyone was called by God to play their unique role and he delighted in their unique worth. God's delight spilled over into the human relationships and each one recognised the other's specialness to God in a mutuality of respect and delight. The holy family was, in fact, a superb icon of God the Trinity who is a perfect relationship of three persons, none of whom is superior to the others, delighting to exchange themselves in love.

This non-hierarchical view of relationships is the one which Paul is struggling to give expression to in his passages about household order such as Ephesians 5.21-33. Everyone has been made equal through the redeeming love of Christ and so everyone must be recognised as such (Galatians 3.28). Many women feel uncomfortable with the hierarchical forms of church government because they contradict this mutuality principle of the gospel.

In the past, the church's teaching has tended to emphasise Ephesians 5 (and not with its implication of mutuality!) as if it is the only New Testament teaching on gender roles, whereas the holy family provides another model. With that thought in mind, I want to look in particular at Joseph who challenges the stereotypes of male-female subordination. If the traditional 'feminine' role has been to be self-effacing in the background, then in that household it was Joseph who fulfilled that feminine role. Joseph is a very special person because in him the two major biblical images of God come together; he was the man in whose face Jesus first glimpsed something of the heavenly Father's face and the man whose loving faithfulness taught Mary what her true husband was like. He acts as an icon in these two ways, pointing both Jesus and Mary towards God and therefore encouraging them both to be obedient to their callings.

Mary is spoken to first by God and initially Joseph is hurt and bewildered by what she has said (Matthew 1.18-25). But then Joseph is spoken to by the Lord and he surrenders himself to his calling, a large part of which is to be the support and partner of Mary. Their relationship is the enfleshed expression of covenant love which she already enjoys with her maker who is her husband. Although her primary obedience and love is for God, she must have known that man's physical presence and support to have been God's gift to her on many occasions,

To look at the holy family is to see a family who knew that each one of them was to be about the Father's business for him- or herself. To look at Joseph in particular is to see a man who was not afraid to be submitted totally to God even if that meant taking second place to his child and wife. It is to see a masculinity which is neither oppressively autocratic in its domination nor so weak and ineffective as to be emasculated. As women, who feel that they have been neglected for much of the church's two-thousand-year history, become more prominent, both men and women will do well to ponder on the much neglected Joseph's role. He may very well develop into one of the most important icons of the future church.

8
The Figure of Wisdom

The fact that Joseph was spoken to by God through a dream is a further challenge to men. The language of dreams comes from the unconscious, a part of the human personality which can seem to be very dangerous and disturbing to many people but (at the risk of another stereotype!) particularly to men. Dreams are not logical but depend on trusting instincts and intuitions which cannot be proved. Since the Enlightenment, it is rational thought which has prevailed in the West and this instinctive knowledge has been dismissed as second-best or even downright wrong.

Yet many women do find it easier to 'think' in terms of gut feelings rather than intellectual logic. They would prefer to use pictures and symbols rather than words to express themselves and they tell stories rather than analyse philosophically. In order to claim their feminine heritage women's groups both inside and outside the church have sought to reverse the imbalance by emphasising intuition and emotions. This can, of course, be equally as dangerous as an over-emphasis on reason. Ironically, it is also dangerously sexist because it can reinforce the impression that women cannot be logical!

This whole question of how women know and experience is so complex that we cannot do anything but make reference to it, but it seems important at least to do that in such a booklet as this. The biblical teaching is actually that neither of these polarisations are the true way of knowing. That comes through wisdom, always described as a female figure. She experiences in a way with which many women identify:

Wisdom knows
> the beginning and end and middle of times,
> the alternation of the solstices
> and the changes of the seasons,
> the cycles of the year and the constellation of the stars,
> the natures of animals and the tempers of wild animals,
> the powers of spirits and the thoughts of human beings,
> the varieties of plants and the virtues of roots.
> (Wisdom of Solomon 7.17-22)

These are the very attributes which many secular women's groups emphasise as they reclaim their female heritage. Indeed, the wisdom figure has in many such groups been claimed as a female saviour with which women can identify, and wisdom is sought as the pinnacle of human experience. However, the biblical view of wisdom is subtly different, for although she is an attribute of human personality, there is no doubt that she derives from the transcendent God and can only be received through grace.

> But I perceived that I would not possess wisdom unless God gave her to me—and it was a mark of insight to know whose gift she was.
>
> (Wisdom of Solomon 8.21)

To be true to women's experience, the church would do well to renew an appreciation of the natural rhythms of the year. These are, of course, picked up by the liturgical year but I would suggest that the connections between the two should be more strongly made. In my own spiritual journey, for example, I have learned from the Celtic Christian tradition to celebrate St Brigid's Day on February 1st, the day which was also the traditional festival of the return of Spring. St Brigid is the patron saint of midwives and her day, followed by Candlemas (February 2nd), the presentation of Christ in the Temple, resonates deeply for me because the imagery of birthing in both festivals feels so much more powerful because it happens at the time when the natural world is also beginning to spring forth. However, it is not only the return of light at the beginning of the year with which I identify but the interplay of the darkness and light. February is still a dark time of the year. The light breaks into that darkness rather than replacing it instantaneously.

This raises a very important question. According to some women's studies, Christianity is irredeemably masculine because its imagery reinforces the idea that anything which happens in the dark is evil whereas that which happens in the light is good. This contrasts with matriarchal religions which tended to be moon-centred. Moonlight is mellow and softens our perspective so that things feel more interconnected than they do in the clear but harsh light of the sun. I do know women who have felt the need to turn to alternative religions precisely because there they have found affirmation for their basic instinct that darkness is beautiful and creative. Women know that growth happens in the dark hiddenness of the womb, through dreams which we dare to listen to when our logic is asleep, in the apparent barrenness of the winter soil as seeds are germinating and in the apparent brokenness of the dark times of life.

This does seem to be a real Joppa issue because for many Christians to enter into such language could be as alarming as for Peter to eat that which he had always believed to be unclean. Yet St Francis celebrated the 'silver moon with softer gleam' and I believe that we must pay heed to some of the ancient wisdoms associated with 'her'. As I have commented previously, this is about being sensitive to female psychology; it is not a theological statement.

Theology, however, is also very important in this area and not just in an academic sense. Darkness may well be a time of slow growth. It can also be a cover for sinister activity. Wise discernment is needed to tell the difference between the two. A male colleague once commented to me that he feels that God is calling more and more women to deliverance ministry and a confrontation with evil precisely because 'you have a different way of looking at things. And you use your instincts to tell whether someone's dark side is from the depths of psychology, or simply evil actions and desires.' I would certainly advise that it is imperative for both men and women to be involved together in such ministry in order for as wide as possible discernment to be employed.

The turning of the seasons reminds us that women's body rhythms are cyclical. (It is precisely because the ancient moon-centred religions reflect the menstrual cycle that many women find them so satisfying.) Our way of knowing reflects this, for women tend not to be linear in their thinking. In particular, we make connections between things rather than compartmentalizing into separated categories. Women appear to be natural weavers who can take several subjects or activities and hold them all together in a way which does not deny the particularity of each thread but recognises their unity. The biblical figure of wisdom is a complex figure. At times she is described as an aspect of God and at times as part of the human response to God. Perhaps the easiest way to identify her is to say that she represents the intimate involvement of God with creation and with humanity in particular. We need to discover the fulness of the biblical teaching about her (and that necessarily includes the Apocrypha) and encourage women to become more confident in her as a role model. Then in their very femininity they will become icons of the femininity of God.

9
Tamar

In contrast, rhythm and balance are not features in the story of another woman, Tamar. I include it because many women find the stereotype of femininity being about calm receptivity deeply offensive and oppressive.

Her story is told in Genesis 38. Tamar had been married to the eldest two of Judah's sons but was left widowed. Under Jewish custom, she should then have been married to the next brother but he was too young. Her father-in-law told her to wait until he was grown up and then they could marry. The years passed and Judah did not fulfil his promise. So, Tamar dressed as a harlot and allowed herself to be seduced by Judah who was unaware of her real identity. Three months later, her pregnancy having been discovered, she was condemned to death by Judah for harlotry. Without accusing him directly, she produced various items which he had given to her. Judah, realising the identity of the harlot with whom he had slept, acknowledged that 'She is more righteous than I inasmuch as I did not give her to my son Shelah.'

Whatever we may think of such a custom, within the culture of that time it was a way of protecting the rights of women—rights that Tamar had been denied. That injustice was made worse by the hypocrisy of a patriarchy which was clearly exercising a double standard of sexual behaviour (it is all right for the men to use harlots but it is not all right for women to be harlots).

Many women today feel similarly trapped by injustices of various kinds, not least by the way that the church has ignored their point of view. The injustice makes them angry but many Christian women have problems with anger. They feel guilty, unfeminine or unforgiving for feeling angry. Yet if the injustices continue, unexpressed rage simply makes them feel worse.

Several women have told me of going to different charismatic prayer meetings in recent months when, as the Holy Spirit came to bless the people, women started to cry and scream. At first they assumed that something demonic was being dealt with but then they realised that the moaning was of repressed pain and anger finally being expressed openly. At one healing weekend the leader had spoken of God sending the Spirit to heal the church of misogyny. When the ministry began and women started to scream he ordered the men to keep away. 'Don't try and touch them yet. There will come a time when they can be ministered to by men. But at the moment they need to held by other women and just given the freedom to be women.' Those who told me such stories all added that, as the ministry continued, they realised that they had so much hurt and rage that had to be got out of their system before they could move on. Often that pain was caused by memories of all kinds of abuse during their childhood. Sometimes it was the frustration

21

of being trapped in relationships where they could not be themselves.

They are all reasonably 'consciousness raised' women and yet they all assumed that such moanings must come from an evil source. I suspect that such a reaction comes from the personal dis-ease many women have about expressing anger combined with the teaching that to be truly womanly is to be passive and silent. It is hardly surprising that others, who are not so aware about women's issues, should dismiss raging women as evil.

This highlights what I have come to see is one of the most important points the church needs to hear about women's perspectives. Women find it easy to believe that they must confess their failings and forgive those who have wronged them. They find it far harder to believe that the person who has wronged them needs to ask their forgiveness. A woman poignantly recalled the prayer time which had brought out one of her very first memories of being hurt as a child. Her counsellor asked her to imagine Jesus in that scene. 'What is Jesus doing?' she was asked. 'He is forgiving my Daddy,' was her instant reply. 'What is he actually doing?' the counsellor persisted. 'He is reaching out his arms to cuddle me.'

I have come to see that the aspect of the gospel with which women really struggle is to believe that 'God is on my side'. Even those who have learned to express their own anger find it easier to do that than to believe that God is angry on their behalf for what has happened. On a very practical level, as a result of listening to women's experience, I never offer a prayer of confession without including some reference to sins committed against us just as I never confess the sin of pride without also acknowledging the sin of self-deprecation! Feeling guilty is not something that women have a problem with but they do need to hear that they are not responsible for all the sins that have been committed.

The story of Tamar reminds us that sin is not only what we do to others but what we have done against us. If you are the victim of injustice then sometimes you are forced into a position of behaving badly or unsubmissively to get your own rights recognised. That applies equally on a level of society and in personal relationships. It does not necessarily mean that your behaviour is beyond reproach but it does mean that you may be more sinned against than sinning. It is to Judah's credit that, without any force, he acknowledged that fact about Tamar.

The fact that she is included as one of the women in the Messianic line (Matthew 1.3) must also remind us that the Saviour who was born in Bethlehem came not only for those who were morally righteous but for the unrighteous. He came also to confront the injustices of society which make it easier for some to be righteous. The church also stands under that confronting judgement and needs to hear that Jesus is angered at structures and behaviour that do not allow women to be their true selves.

10
Jezebel

My final icon is Jezebel—and it is but a quick snapshot of her. Her very name is now used to refer to a scheming temptress and murderess which is the very stereotype which women have reacted against. I include her to say that there is some truth in the stereotype! Women are as capable of hurting and destroying men as the other way round. We may stand at another Joppa but the gospel message remains the same today as it did then. We are all equally sinners and equally in need of knowing the redeeming love of Jesus Christ.

11
Further Reading

There are so many books on the issues raised by this booklet that it would be impossible to give a comprehensive list. I am therefore highlighting five which, between them, cover most of the topics.

The person of Mary is dealt with more fully than I have been able to in Elaine Storkey's *Mary's Story, Mary's Song* (Fount 1993). Her place within Christian tradition is dealt with more theologically in Max Thurian's *Mary, Mother of the Lord, Figure of the Church* (Mowbrays 1963).

The image of God as husband is considered in my own *For Your Maker Is Your Husband* (Epworth 1991).

The title of Andrew Doze's *Discovering St Joseph* (St Paul Publications 1989) is self-explanatory.

When it comes to the literature about feminine consciousness, it is difficult to know what books to recommend, partly because there are so many and partly because most are only good in parts. However, I do want to pick out one which, in my experience, has spoken to every woman who has read it: Clarissa Pinkola Este's *Women who Run With the Wolves: Liberating the Wild Woman Archetype* (Rider Books 1992). Its intriguing title comes from the author's observation of the similarity between the instinctiveness of wolves and women and how both have been accused of being devious and devouring!

12
Questions for Further Thought

1. What are the implications for the ministry in acknowledging that 'feminine' and 'masculine' traits are shared by men and women in varying proportions?
2. Which parts of church life appeal to masculine traits and which to the feminine?
3. What stories can you think of from history which would make good icons of women's contribution to history?
4. If churches, generally, are perceived as having 'hierarchical' forms of church government, what would local church leadership patterns look like if they were more inclusive of 'feminine' traits or more mutually submissive in character?
5. If people are turning to the 'New Age' or secular feminism out of frustration with the church, how do Christians need to change to allow a fuller expression of that which is authentic to the feminine?
6. How can we help to foster 'midwife'-style ministries?
7. From earliest times, God has revealed a better way' which has provided people with a different way from those of the surrounding pagans. This has happened in missionary work down through the centuries. With the re-emergence of many pagan ideas, how can we transform them into a better way under the hand of God?
8. Do you find that sexuality is celebrated in your church? What is its attitude to being married and being single? Does the icon of Ruth and Boaz say anything new to you?
9. What experiences have you had when 'darkness' has been creative and beautiful?
10. The icon of Tamar reminds us of the way that those who have power (in this case, men) use it to perpetuate distorted values ('it is all right for men to use harlots but not for women to be harlots'). Can you think of other contemporary examples of this?
11. In what ways is Joseph a good role model for
    a) men
    b) husbands
    c) fathers?